GERMAN FIGHTERS OVER THE MED

This is a photograph well worth prolonged examination. It shows a Bf 110D-1/U1 night fighter of I/NJG 3 which was formed from LG 1 in the summer of 1941, and for a short while operated in the Mediterranean theatre. Aircraft code is L1 + DH and it appears to be black overall. However, closer examination shows that the port undercarriage doors are a lighter colour as are the under surface of the port tailplane and the port fin. There is also a white tactical band around the top half only of the rear fuselage. The owl and half moon insignia on the nose is the unit badge of I/NJG 1 (435/1016A/4).

BRYAN PHILPOTT
GERMAN FIGHTERS OVER THE MED

WORLD WAR 2 PHOTO ALBUM

A selection of German wartime photographs from the Bundesarchiv, Koblenz

AZTEX Corporation, Tucson, AZ

© 1981 Patrick Stephens Ltd.

German Fighters over the Mediterranean

Library of Congress Catalog Number 81-065149

ISBN 0-89404-048-0

Published by AZTEX Corporation

First published in 1980
Patrick Stephens, Ltd.
Bar Hill, Cambridge
England, CB3 8EL

AZTEX Corporation
Tucson, Arizona 85703

Printed in the United States of America

CONTENTS

CAMPAIGN MAP 6
AUTHOR'S INTRODUCTION 7
ABOUT THE PHOTOGRAPHS 14
THE PHOTOGRAPHS 15
APPENDICES 94

Acknowledgements
The author and publisher would like to express their sincere thanks to Dr Matthias Haupt and Herr Meinrad Nilges of the Bundesarchiv for their assistance, without which this book would have been impossible.

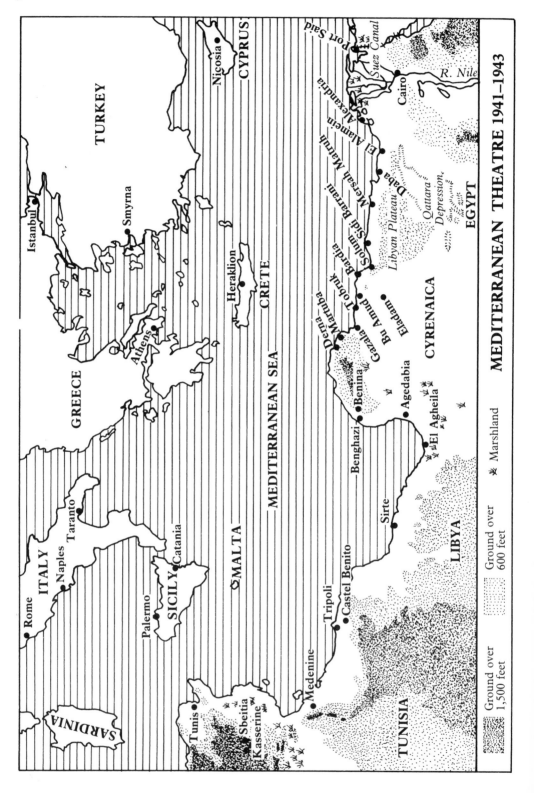

MEDITERRANEAN THEATRE 1941–1943

The strategic importance of the Mediterranean was not overlooked by the British when war broke out in 1939. But with the Straits of Gibraltar in their control at one end and the Suez Canal at the other, there was little need for alarm. Indeed the only real threat to the security of the area appeared to come from the Italians, who to all intents and purposes were still very much on the sidelines, seemingly playing a waiting game while their armed forces were being modernised. During the so-called Phoney War the RAF built up a small but efficient air force in the Middle East which, due to demands in other theatres, had a very low priority on men and equipment. Nonetheless RAF Middle East had enough resources to defend areas of major importance as well as to provide bases from which bomber and reconnaissance aircraft could operate. The only area neglected was the island of Malta where only a token force of Sea Gladiators based at Hal Far provided fighter defence.

Although Hitler was aware of the importance of the Mediterranean, it did not feature prominently in his early plans which, even while the Battle of Britain was in progress, included a major assault on the Russians in the east. The success of the German Blitzkrieg which began on May 10 1940, and quickly resulted in the occupation of Northern France, the Low Countries and the rout of the British Expeditionary Force, directly resulted in a reappraisal of Hitler's priorities, as well as a token weakening of the forces available to him.

The successful campaign in France led Mussolini to believe that victory would soon be Germany's and if he wanted to share the spoils of war he must act immediately. Consequently, on June 10 he declared war on the Allies and marched into Southern France. Mussolini's plans to turn the Mediterranean into an area completely dominated by Italy were grandiose to say the least. His air force was numerically strong but lacked modern equipment or know-how, and his land forces were little better. Thus, there was no way they could hope to achieve the success he envisaged in a long drawn out campaign, and they did not have the expertise to accomplish a quick victory. Initial successes in Southern France, North Africa and the Balkans gave a false sense of achievement. However, by December mammoth losses in Libya, Greece and Egypt forced Hitler into increasing his material help as it was necessary to protect his important southern flank which featured prominently in his Russian plans.

Since June 1940 the Luftwaffe had been helping the Italians with a liaison force under the command of General Ritter von Pohl, but this was mainly confined to the transportation of troops. No Luftwaffe combat units in the form of bomber or fighter squadrons appeared on the scene until December when the first elements of Generalmajor Hans Geisler's Fliegerkorps X arrived in Sicily. Geisler faced a task of massive proportions with a force totalling only some 350 aircraft, of which initially only III/ZG 76 equipped with Bf 110Cs was a fighter unit. But at this time fighters were not his main priority, since the German plan to redress the balance was based on their previous success with lightning strikes by dive-bombers supported by conventional bombing.

Although Hitler did not want to become too involved at this time in the Middle East war, he knew that the occupation of Crete by the British, which occurred as a result of the Italian advance on Greece, and the precarious position of the Italians in Albania, seriously threatened his plans. Consequently, in addition to Fliegerkorps X which he hoped would retrieve the situation in the Balkans, he also sent two Panzer divisions to North Africa. The avoidance of a long campaign was essential if Germany's major plans were to proceed, and the only way to achieve this objective was to close the Mediterranean to the British, thus denying supplies to their forces in the eastern extremities of the area. The key to this was the island of Malta, a refuelling and refuge point for allied convoys, warships and aircraft. While plans were afoot to mount a massive aerial assault on the island, the Luftwaffe moved supplies and technicians into Italy to prepare bases. They were therefore committed to an air war on two fronts at a time when efforts should have been made to conserve strength for the planned assault on the Soviet Union.

Geisler set up his headquarters in the Hotel Domenico in Taormina and commenced carrying out the three major tasks his force had been assigned: 1) an offensive against Malta; 2) control the straits between Tunis and Sicily; and 3) assist the Italians with air support in North Africa and eventually obtain air superiority to enable safe transport of supplies and men to North Africa. In addition to the major objectives the small force available to Geisler was also expected to attack any reinforcements heading for and using the Suez Canal.

From January to March Fliegerkorps X mounted a continuous assault on Malta and in so doing suffered heavy losses at the hands of the ground defences, the few fighters based on the island, and the carrier-borne reinforcements. Until the arrival of 7/JG 26 under the command of Oberleutnant Müncheberg and I/JG 27 under Hauptmann Neumann, fighter escort was in the hands of the Bf 110s of ZG 26. The two Jagdgeschwadern were both equipped with Bf 109E-7 aircraft which were superior to the defending Hurricanes. In fact, one of these British fighters fell to the guns of Müncheberg on February 12, just three days after 7/JG 26 arrived in Sicily. In addition to escort duties the Bf 109s also carried out strafing attacks against land and sea targets accounting for a considerable quantity of Wellingtons, Sunderlands and Maryland reconnaissance bombers.

By March 1941 the Luftwaffe had virtually achieved its objective as far as Malta was concerned for, although the defenders had taken a very heavy toll of German bombers, especially Ju 87s, the island was virtually untenable as far as offensive aircraft were concerned, and all Wellingtons, Sunderlands and the like were withdrawn. Having managed to gain some form of air superiority over Malta the Luftwaffe handed back responsibility to the Italians and by the end of May all Luftwaffe units, apart from a Staffel of Ju 88 reconnaissance aircraft, had been withdrawn. During its three-month sojourn 7/JG 26 claimed 42 victories in the Malta campaign, of which Oberleutnant Joachim Müncheberg was credited with 20.

This part of JG 26 moved to North Africa to reinforce the units already there, in support of what was eventually to become known as the Afrika Korps. I/JG 27, which for a very short time had shared escort duties

over Malta with 7/JG 26, continued its nomadic career by also moving to North Africa, while its other elements, Stab, II and III Gruppen, moved to Bulgarian airfields to join General Alois Löhr's Luftflotte 4 in the Balkans campaign.

Allied aircraft in the form of Hurricanes, Wellingtons, Blenheims and Gladiators had been taking an increasing interest in targets around Albania, and the Italian air force suffered heavy losses in trying to gain air superiority. On April 6 1941 the Luftwaffe mounted simultaneous assaults on Greece and Yugoslavia under the code name Operation Marita. The tactics which they employed had proved successful in every campaign except the one waged against the British Isles. The main assault was led by Ju 87s followed by Do 17s and He 111s, all escorted by Bf 109Es and Fs of JG 26, JG 27, JG 54, JG 77 and 1(J)LG 2. One of the latter unit's pilots, Leutnant Giesshardt, opened his account with four Hawker Fury biplanes of the Royal Yugoslavian Air Force which he destroyed in one sortie on the opening day. In the northern sector JG 54 were engaged in a rather bizarre encounter when they were attacked by Hurricanes and Bf 109Es of the RYAF, but in their superior Bf 109Fs managed to overcome the combination of what were normally opposing aircraft.

The only serious losses to the Luftwaffe fighter units occurred when 111/JG 27 were surprised by Hurricanes of No 33 Squadron and lost five of their Bf 109s in the ensuing conflict.

Air superiority was gained in a very short space of time and by April 20 Athens was under attack from Ju 88s and Do 17s escorted by Bf 110s of II/ZG 26 and Bf 109s of II/JG 27, both units taking a heavy toll of the RAF Hurricanes which attempted to intercept the bombers. The Bf 109s and 110s were used in strafing sorties which had proved so successful in Malta, and they accounted for a number of Blenheims which were flying personnel to Crete.

The end of the campaign in Greece and Yugoslavia secured Hitler's southern flank and most of the units involved were withdrawn to take part in the invasion of Russia, which no doubt would have been mounted sooner if the Italians had not needed the help of the Luftwaffe.

In just under a year from the time Italy entered the war, the Allied armies and air forces had been forced to evacuate the whole

9

European continent, and now had only a very tenuous hold on the island of Crete; a hold which was soon to be removed by one of the major paratroop operations of World War 2.

With a large proportion of the German air force withdrawn for the proposed invasion of Russia, the only fighter units remaining with Fliegerkorps VIII for Operation Mercury – the invasion of Crete – were I and II/ZG 26 with Bf 110Cs and I, II and III Gruppen of JG 77 with Bf 109Es, the five Gruppen between them mustering some 180 fighters. The air assault of the island opened on May 3 when 24 Ju 88s of I and II/LG 1 opened the first of a series of attacks designed to secure the airfields. Allied fighters took a toll of the unescorted German and Italian bombers but their success was to be short-lived, for soon the Bf 109s and 110s, together with Italian fighters, brought considerable pressure to bear on the defenders.

All the advantages lay with the German fighter pilots: they had better equipment, no fuel or ammunition problems and, if they were shot down into the sea, stood a very good chance of rescue by their own side. Against this the defending pilots were flying tired Hurricanes and obsolete Gladiators; fuel and ammunition supplies were acute and replenishment was fraught with danger since supply ships could only reach the island from Libya and Egypt by running the gauntlet of aerial attack by Italian torpedo bombers. By May 20 the Luftwaffe fighter pilots had reduced the defending fighter force to four Hurricanes and three Gladiators, which were evacuated to Egypt only hours before the main aerial assault.

By the end of May, Crete was in German hands and the whole picture in the Mediterranean looked entirely different from the year before. Credit for the success belonged to the Luftwaffe units which had been available in a variety of strengths wherever they were needed. Air-to-air combat involving fighters did not rival the epic battles of France or Britain, but once again the German fighter pilots had proved that they were a match for anyone, and their aircraft were, at that time, far better than any the Allies had in the theatre.

While the activity in Greece, Malta and Crete had been occupying the generals and tacticians, just across the Mediterranean in North Africa other events had been following a somewhat more subdued, but none

the less important, course. During December 1940 the British had set out with the intention of occupying all territories then in the hands of the Italians and on the 9th of the month opened a major offensive aimed at Sidi Barrani. Success followed success and Cyrenaica with its capital of Benghazi was wrested from the Italians. But in February 1941 the advance elements of Rommel's Afrika Korps arrived to add support to the faltering Italians. The Germans were quick to take advantage of the stretched British supply lines and by March 12 had retaken El Agheila and mounted a major offensive causing British retreats, which by April 15 had resulted in the encirclement of Tobruk.

In the opening days of the Afrika Korps' campaign aerial support had consisted of Henschel 126 reconnaissance/light bombers and approximately 18 Bf 110Cs of III/ZG 26 which acted as fighters and in ground-attack roles. The 110s scored their first success over the RAF on February 19 when two Hurricanes of No 3 Squadron were shot down; seemingly a reversal of fortunes, for over England and France the heavy German twin had been no match for the Hurricane. But in this case the single-engined British fighters were in the hands of new pilots who had just converted from Gladiators, and were pitched against Bf 110 veterans. The German fighters gave able support in the ground-attack role, but were often called into action against Blenheims and Hurricanes which were harassing the advancing ground forces.

In mid-April the Bf 110s were reinforced by the arrival of three Staffeln of I/JG 27 which was still under the command of Hauptmann Eduard Neumann, and flying tropicalised versions of the Bf 109E–4. Operating from their airfield at Ain El Gazala (which they later shared with 7/JG 26 also flying Bf 109E–4s and 2(H)14 with Hs 126s), Oberleutnant Redlich's 1 Staffel was in action on April 19 claiming four Hurricanes of which two fell to the guns of the Staffelkäpitan. But two days later when escorting Ju 87s to Tobruk JG 27 lost two Bf 109s to defending Hurricanes which also accounted for three Stukas. However, on April 23 two Blenheims and five Hurricanes fell to the 109s and among the victorious Luftwaffe pilots was Oberfähnrich Joachim Marseille, who was to become a legend in his own lifetime and the leading 'ace' in the Western desert.

In one of the biggest air battles of the

desert war up to that time, practically all of I/JG 27's 34 serviceable Bf 109s, supported by ten Bf 110s of III/ZG 26, escorted 20 Ju 87s of II/StG 2 on April 23 against the beleaguered Tobruk. Four Hurricanes were shot down but their colleagues accounted for two of the 109s and four dive-bombers, and later in the day another Bf 109 was lost.

During May the British, who had withdrawn two of their fighter squadrons, lost only 15 aircraft, five of which were Blenheims all accounted for in one action by 3/JG 27 on the 21st of the month. These decreased losses were due to a respite in aerial activity as both sides built up their strengths to await further developments on the ground. These were not long in coming with a renewed British attempt to relieve the garrison at Tobruk. The Allied air force now had a fighter strength of five Hurricane-equipped squadrons and one with Curtiss Tomahawks, the remainder of their air strength comprising Wellingtons, Marylands, Blenheims and Baltimores. Against this total of some 150 aircraft the Luftwaffe could muster 41 Bf 109s and 25 Bf 110s of which an average of 36 were serviceable at any one time.

Pilots of the German fighters were much more experienced than their Allied counterparts, who now consisted of young South Africans, Australians, New Zealanders as well as newly arrived RAF pilots. The action aimed at recovering Tobruk and code-named Battle Axe failed as British ground forces were decimated by the Africa Korps whose 88 mm anti-tank weapon destroyed a large number of the 8th Army's Crusader and Valentine tanks. In the air the situation was little better with the experienced German pilots accounting for 33 British fighters in the three-day campaign. By June 18 Battle Axe had failed and the British had withdrawn to the borders of Egypt to reform.

Aerial activity in the following months continued at a less furious pace but wherever Allied aircraft appeared there always seemed to be some Bf 109s to oppose them. More often than not the nimble German fighter was in the hands of an ace pilot such as Müncheberg, Lippert or Marseille, the latter having reached 23 victories by the end of September including five in one day on September 24.

Sporadic activity in the air between June and September 1941 served only to underline the apparent stalemate on the ground but,

beneath the seemingly calm acceptance of the situation by both sides, strengths were being built up for further action.

Rommel's aim was finally to take Tobruk, thus leaving the way open for him to advance into Egypt. During his build-up the Luftwaffe had not been neglected and, although General Hoffman von Waldau's Fliegerführer Afrika, which had been formed in June, had only been increased by a small amount, the quality had improved. Worried by the new RAF aircraft being introduced into the area, the fighter pilots had been pressing for later marks of the Bf 109 and in September they were rewarded when the F version started to arrive. The first to be equipped was I/JG 27 who were later joined in North Africa by II/JG 27 which had seen action in Russia and Greece before returning to Germany to convert to Bf 109F–4s.

The newly arrived Gruppe took their F models into action for the first time on October 3 losing one of their number but claiming three British fighters. To counter British night raids against supply ports, I/NJG 3 with their Bf 110 night fighters had been moved to Derna from Europe, but in October they were recalled to help combat the growing threat of RAF Bomber Command's night raids. In early November six Ju 88C–6 night fighters of 2/NJG 2 took over the specialist role. On November 18 1941 the British launched their counter-offensive, Operation Crusader, and in so doing caught Rommel by surprise before he had time to mount his own offensive. In the following weeks the 190 aircraft of Fliegerführer Afrika were to come in for a lot of hard work, a great deal of it falling on the shoulders of the fighter pilots.

The first objective of the German pilots was to achieve air superiority over the battlegrounds and, although the opening days of the campaign saw them frustrated by bad weather, they had only to wait until November 22 to meet the revitalised British fighters in a battle the outcome of which would decide the whole future strategy of the fighter in the desert war.

During the action on November 22 the German fighter pilots found that a well-handled Tomahawk was a much tougher proposition than a Hurricane. However, at the end of the day, JG 27 claimed 13 fighters and eight bombers for the loss of five Bf 109s, a rate very much in their favour but one which the numerically inferior Luftwaffe could not afford to withstand on a regular basis. The following day nine more British fighters were claimed as well as one bomber, making a haul for the two days of 22 fighters and nine bombers, figures which were later substantiated as ten fighters and four bombers. During the fighting on the 23rd, JG 27 lost one more Bf 109; a loss they felt very keenly as the pilot was Hauptmann Lippert, the Gruppen Commander of II/JG 27. Lippert managed to bale out of his crippled aircraft but succumbed to his injuries in an Egyptian hospital on December 3 1941.

The difficulties faced by the German fighter pilots in trying to match a numerically superior enemy were brought home to them during these two air battles, and it was obvious that they could not hope to survive for long with the rate of attrition suffered. From this point on their tactics had to be to avoid direct air-to-air combat with Allied fighters, but to use the superior performance of their Bf 109Fs to break up escort fighter squadrons and attack the bombers which were hammering the Afrika Korps almost at will. Although the fighters continued to take a heavy toll of Allied aircraft, analysis of the desert campaign clearly shows that it was in late 1941 that the Luftwaffe fighter squadrons started to concede superiority to the Allied air force.

The British push on the ground did not succeed in knocking out Rommel's armour, and fortunes once again swung the German leader's way in January 1942 when Benghazi was retaken. This was a remarkable achievement for by this time serviceability among the Luftwaffe units was very poor and the ground forces received very little support. For example, in January JG 27 could only put into the air 24 aircraft and consequently the sortie rate deteriorated and remained poor for three months. Despite this, those pilots who flew continued to achieve success, none more than Marseille, who by now had been commissioned and in April was made Staffelkäpitan of 3/JG 27. This remarkable man, well supported by his wingman – an essential ingredient in any fighter pilot's success story – continued to claim victim after victim. His score stood at 91 on June 4 1942 when he was awarded the Knight's Cross and Oakleaves, and 12 days later he passed his century before taking a well-earned leave. On his return to the arena he was to achieve a remarkable feat which was supported by eye-witnesses from both sides and substantiated by official British loss records. On September 1 Marseille took off for his first action at 0730 hours; by 1755 hours he had flown three sorties and had personally accounted for 17 Allied aircraft, an achievement unmatched in the annals of aerial combat.

Naturally enough two days later Marseille received his country's highest award – the Knight's Cross and Oakleaves, Swords and Diamonds – but sadly by the end of the month he was dead. His end came on the last day of September when his Bf 109 caught fire, forcing him to bale out; his parachute did not open, possibly because the 23-year-old ace struck the tailplane and was knocked unconscious but, whatever the reason, Germany had lost one of her most popular and successful pilots. All but seven of his 158 victories were achieved in the Western Desert and they typified the skill and spirit of not only Marseille but all fighter pilots who fought against superior numbers but knew every trick of their chosen trade.

During the lull in action in Libya, eyes were once again turned to Malta for, despite the efforts of the Regia Aeronautica, the British had been rebuilding their strength on the island, especially with fighters, and were now causing serious problems to the supply routes and ports being used to sustain the Afrika Korps.

In late November 1941 Feldmarschall Kesselring had been moved from the Russian Front to Sicily to take command of Fliegerkorps II which was in the process of reforming after heavy losses in the Russian campaign; its fighter units consisted of Stab, I, II and III/JG 53 and II/JG 3, all equipped with Bf 109s. These units were supported by the Bf 110s of III/ZG 26 and I/NJG 2 which operated with Ju 88C–6 fighters.

Kesselring mounted several minor attacks against Malta in the opening months of 1942, but in March a major assault was launched and this was to continue for two months. The story of how Malta was under almost continual attack is now well known and does not need repeating, save to say that fighter pilots on both sides were heavily involved. In mid-May 1942 Kesselring called off his offensive having lost about 500 aircraft of all types during five months' action. The proposed expansion of the war in North Africa and the resumption of the Russian campaign meant that aircraft were needed elsewhere, and the impossibility of trying to fight an air war on three fronts with limited resources was now beginning to become evident to Luftwaffe staff officers. Malta was still under siege and convoys routed to it came under attack from bombers based in Crete and Sicily, but there was very little German fighter action as the units involved were now back in Russia or North Africa.

Rommel opened his new offensive on May 26 and by June 11 had retaken Ben Hacheim, followed ten days later by Tobruk. During this campaign the fighters of JG 53 and JG 27 had given support to the Stukas and Ju 88s, some of which operated from Crete. But by September, Rommel was facing serious problems due to interference with his very long lines of supply. In October Montgomery mounted his counter-offensive at El Alamein, by which time his desert air force totalled more than 700 aircraft, a numerical strength of nearly 3 to 1 against the Luftwaffe. By November 15 only some 100 German fighters of JG 27 and JG 77 remained in the area, the German army was in full retreat, and lack of fuel, ammunition and spares curtailed operations to an ineffective number.

Luftflotte 2 was reinforced during the autumn of 1942 since it was realised that Allied landings would take place to open a second front. Among the units moved from Russia and France to reinforce the Mediterranean theatre were 11/JG 2, 11/JG 26, II/JG 2, I/JG 53 and Stab and III/JG 77. Of these II/JG 2 were equipped with FW 190A-4s and the rest with Bf 109s of various sub-types. Apart from the radial-engined FW 190, another newcomer was the Me 210 which was being operated by a Staffel of III/ZG 1. Operation Torch, the Allied landings in North Africa, commenced on November 8 1942 and from then on supplies were poured into the theatre by the German High Command, but it was all too late. Hurricanes, Spitfires and Beaufighters took a terrible toll of transports and bombers, but they also suffered at the hands of the German fighter pilots who were still a force to be reckoned with, and now encountered new targets in the form of B–17s, P–40s and P–38s of the USAAF.

The B–17s started raiding Tunis on November 16 and were escorted by P–38 Lightnings which, in the main, were flown by inexperienced pilots. Although the American twin-tailed fighter was faster and more heavily armed than the Bf 109, the experienced German pilots soon worked out efficient tactics, and in the early days the Americans lost heavily, especially to II/JG 51. In December both sides suffered heavy losses in the air, the honours going marginally to the German fighters who in one action of the 4th shot down all 11 Bisley bombers sent to attack forward Luftwaffe airfields.

The New Year started with the Germans fighting a rearguard action on the ground but oddly enough the Luftwaffe could still command a large amount of air superiority, a typical example being the practically unmolested roamings of FW 190s and Bf 109s over the area containing the American airfield at Thelepte. However, over the whole front, attrition was high and among those killed was Major Müncheberg of JG 77; to replace men of his experience was very difficult indeed. As the situation in Tunisia deteriorated the Luftwaffe withdrew once again to Sicily from where I and II JG 53 continued to operate over the front for as long as they could.

By May 12 1943 all units of the Luftwaffe were either safe in Sicily, completely wiped out, or captured; the last fighters to evacuate Tunisia being those of JG 77 which left on May 8. During the opening months of the 'Torch' campaign Luftwaffe fighter units had enjoyed considerable success, but in the end sheer weight of numbers, better supplies and superior aircraft inflicted an overwhelming defeat.

Luftflotte 2 assumed responsibility for Sicily, Sardinia and Italy and a new command, Luftwaffenkommando Süd Ost, looked after the interests of Crete, Greece and the Balkans. To counter growing Allied air superiority, priority was given to the build-up of fighter units and, of the 400 aircraft received in the area after the evacuation of Tunisia, more than 220 were fighters. The Germans were at a loss as to the likely site of the first Allied landings and when these occurred in Sicily on July 10 there was little aerial opposition. Softening up by Allied bombers had reduced Luftwaffe fighter serviceability to a frightening level and only a handful of Bf 109s and FW 190s attempted to interfere with Montgomery and Patton's forces.

At this time the Luftwaffe had more or less given up any hope of achieving air superiority and they conceded this to the Allies in August 1943 by withdrawing four fighter

Gruppen from the Mediterranean theatre for the defence of the Reich.

There were several instances during the invasion of Italy when Allied air support was not as good as it might have been, and on such occasions units such as JG 3, JG 53 and JG 77 took full advantage of the situation. They usually operated in the ground-attack role with one unit acting as top cover, but sometimes took part in massed combats with Allied fighters which in many cases were operating at extreme range from airfields in Sardinia.

After the Allied landings at Anzio the overall situation continued to deteriorate for the Luftwaffe. The Jagdgruppen within Luftflotte 2 used their FW 190s and Bf 109s effectively against bridgeheads and targets of opportunity but by the middle of 1944 the Spitfires, P-51s, P-47s and P-38s controlled the skies over Italy and as far as the Luftwaffe was concerned the Mediterranean was a lost cause. Units were withdrawn to bolster those already engaged in the defence of the Reich, and by July 1944 the total Luftwaffe strength in the theatre was down to 300 aircraft.

The hey-day of the German Jagdgruppen in the Middle East had been 1941 and early 1942. During this period they proved that a comparatively small but well-equipped force could achieve and maintain air superiority. But while they were doing this, the writing was already on the wall, for there was no way the Luftwaffe chiefs could fight on three separate fronts, each of which presented its own peculiarities. Credit must not, however, be taken from the fighter pilots whose sole task was to fight and fight well. There can be no doubt that they achieved this to a fine degree in the skies over Malta, Sicily, Greece, Tunisia and Italy.

ABOUT THE PHOTOGRAPHS

The photographs in this book have been selected with care from the Bundesarchiv, Koblenz (the approximate German equivalent of the US National Archives or the British Public Records Office). Particular attention has been devoted to choosing photographs which will be fresh to the majority of readers, although it is inevitable that one or two may be familiar. Other than this, the author's prime concern has been to choose good-quality photographs which illustrate the type of detail that enthusiasts and modellers require. In certain instances quality has, to a degree, been sacrificed in order to include a particularly interesting photograph. For the most part, however, the quality speaks for itself.

The Bundesarchiv files hold some one million black and white negatives of Wehrmacht and Luftwaffe subjects, including 150,000 on the Kriegsmarine, some 20,000 glass negatives from the inter-war period and several hundred colour photographs. Sheer numbers is one of the problems which makes the compilation of a book such as this difficult. Other difficulties include the fact that, in the vast majority of cases, the negatives have not been printed so the researcher is forced to look through box after box of 35 mm contact strips – some 250 boxes containing an average of over 5,000 pictures each, plus folders containing a further 115,000 contact prints of the Waffen-SS; moreover, cataloguing and indexing the negatives is neither an easy nor a short task, with the result that, at the present time, Luftwaffe and Wehrmacht subjects as well as entirely separate theatres of operations are intermingled in the same files.

There is a simple explanation for this confusion. The Bundesarchiv photographs were taken by war correspondents attached to German military units, and the negatives were originally stored in the Reich Propaganda Ministry in Berlin. Towards the close of World War 2, all the photographs – then numbering some $3\frac{1}{2}$ million – were ordered to be destroyed. One man in the Ministry, a Herr Evers, realised that they should be preserved for posterity and, acting entirely unofficially and on his own initiative, commandeered the first available suitable transport – two refrigerated fish trucks – loaded the negatives into them, and set out for safety. Unfortunately, one of the trucks disappeared en route and, to this day, nobody knows what happend to it. The remainder were captured by the Americans and shipped to Washington, where they remained for 20 years before the majority were returned to the government of West Germany. A large number, however, still reside in Washington. Thus the Bundesarchiv files are incomplete, with infuriating gaps for any researcher. Specifically, they end in the autumn of 1944, after Arnhem, and thus record none of the drama of the closing months of the war.

The photographs are currently housed in a modern office block in Koblenz, overlooking the River Mosel. The priceless negatives are stored in the basement, and there are strict security checks on anyone seeking admission to the Bildarchiv (Photo Archive). Regrettably, and the author has been asked to stress this point, the archives are *only open to bona fide authors and publishers, and prints can only be supplied for reproduction in a book or magazine.* They CANNOT be supplied to private collectors or enthusiasts for personal use, so *please* – don't write to the Bundesarchiv or the publishers of this book asking for copy prints, because they cannot be provided. The well-equipped photo laboratory at the Bundesarchiv is only capable of handling some 80 to 100 prints per day because each is printed individually under strictly controlled conditions – another reason for the fine quality of the photographs but also a contributory factor in the above legislation.

Right See page 68.

THE PHOTOGRAPHS

This page When the Allies invaded North Africa the Luftwaffe took control of the Vichy French Air Force. Among the 1,876 aircraft impressed by the Luftwaffe were a total of 246 Dewoitine 520s including these two in Tunisia. Aircraft No 3 belonged to No 248 GC 11/7 4th Escadrille Vichy Air Force (435/1002A/4A and 5a).

Above This Caudron C 445 was used by Luftflotte 2 as a communications aircraft until it came to grief in Southern Italy (432/784/3).
Below The Vichy Air Force also handed over this rather odd-looking Farmann 223-2 carrying the legend S. Lieutenant Casse, probably a reference to the pilot (435/1002/31A).

Above A Bf 109E-7 of an unknown unit in North Africa. The aircraft number on the white fuselage band was not uncommon on 1 Gruppe aircraft in this theatre. Spinner is white and there is also a white band on the under-nose cowling (597/503a/26).

Below Just what these nine pilots of JG 53 are celebrating is unrecorded, but the variety of styles of dress is worthy of note especially as far as footwear is concerned. Also note the tropical filter on the aircraft and the JG 53 Pik As badge (468/1407/3A).

Above Bf 109G-5 of II/JG 53 in Sicily. The man standing by the wing tip is an Italian Air Force officer (468/1404/29A).

Below German aircrew in Italy with SM 79 tri-motor bombers in the background. The men are probably bomber crew as the overall one-piece suit was rarely used by fighter pilots, except for some flying Bf 110s. Life jackets are early kapok-filled type (422/39/2A).

Above Three immaculate Bf 109Gs of JG 53 under temporary camouflage at their base in Sicily (468/1403/28).

Below JG 27 is one of the most famous units associated with North Africa. A Bf 109E-4 of this unit is seen in Sicily en route to North Africa. Note the long-range centre-line tank and European camouflage with the top of the yellow (04) cowling oversprayed (428/482/32).

Above Bf 109G-6/R2 with 21 cm Wfr Gr 21 mortar tubes under the wings. It is from an unknown unit operating in Italy (469/1492/6).

Below The ground crew of this Bf 109G of the Gruppe Adjutant of JG 77 relax in the Italian sunshine in 1944. The camouflage netting over the wings, and that on the fuselage supported by the aircraft's aerial, is of interest, as is the pilot's helmet which can be seen hanging in the open cockpit (473/1836/16).

Background photograph This pair (Rotte) of Bf 109E-4Ns of I/JG 27 are probably the most photographed 109s of World War 2. No excuse is made for reproducing yet another view as it clearly shows how the top surface sand (79) colour, blotched with brownish green (80), merged with the desert. Under-surface colour was light blue (78) (435/1006A/26A).

Below inset Bf 109E-7 of JG 26 has its centre-line 66-gallon fuel tank filled up, whilst another crew man cleans the windscreen. Cowling is yellow (04) as is the tip of the spinner (432/761/31).

Below right inset Contrasting forms of transport. The Bf 109F-2 Trop belongs to 3/JG 53 and has 74/75/76 camouflage with a white spinner and fuselage band. The figure 8 is yellow, edged in black. The two mules and their owner originate from Tunisia where the photograph was taken in 1943 (419/1898/7A).

Above A pilot of JG 51 leaves his Bf 109G on which the European camouflage and tropical filter are prominent. The pilot is wearing a late-style inflatable life jacket and lightweight over-trousers over his summer dress uniform (468/1414/13A).

Left Port fin/rudder of the same Bf 110D-3 showing eight kills, all of which are RAF aircraft. Battle damage has been patched and doped with red oxide. The number W.N. 3412, forward of the Swastika, is the aircraft's Werke Nr (422/32/23a).

Above This Bf 110D-3 is probably the aircraft of Feldwebel Günther Wegman of III/ZG 26. Colour scheme is 74/75/76 and the photograph clearly shows the extended fuselage tail-cone of this version of the Bf 110 which housed a dinghy (422/32/24a).

Right More kill markings. This time the 50th victory of Hans-Joachim Marseille, probably the most famous ace to come out of the desert campaign. Aircraft is a Bf 109F-2 Trop and the rudder is red. Overall camouflage was sand (79) with Hellblau (65) under surfaces. The pilot watching the painting is Marseille (440/1373/31).

Above Full flap, gear down, engine idling, as this Bf 109G-2 approaches to land over yellow 8 of 6/JG 27 and an Opel BLITZ truck (421/2070/12).

Left The game seems to have reached a critical stage for these Bf 109 pilots of JG 77 in Italy. The aircraft is an F-2. All pilots are wearing over-trousers and inflatable life jackets on which the automatic inflating cylinder can be seen on the two standing pilots (565/1405/26).

Above right Bf 110G-2 of II/ZG 1 carrying the famous Wespen Geschwader nose art. This aircraft operated from Italy in the summer of 1943 (468/1436/15).

Centre right A Bf 110E-2 of III/ZG 26. This is a Stab aircraft and the individual letter D is in green. The ZG 26 badge is a red ladybird on a white diamond. This aircraft is finished in 74/75/76 and also has the long tail-cone housing a dinghy (422/25/13A).

Right This Bf 109E of JG 27 has an empty ETC fuselage rack which might indicate that it has just returned from a bombing support role (431/707/39).

Above left Marseille in the cockpit of his Bf 109F-2 Trop 'Gelb 14'. The aircraft is finished sand (79) overall on top surfaces and Hellblau (65) underneath. The figure 14 is in yellow (04) (439/1271/35).

Left Another variation of individual aircraft marking on a Bf 109E of III/JG 27. This time the figure is painted directly on to the white cowling, and is black with a white outline (429/622/29).

Above Bf 109E-4B of III/JG 27 having a bomb loaded on to its centre-line rack. The aircraft has a white cowling on which its individual figure 2 has been painted yellow outlined in black on a camouflaged disc (429/622/9).

Right The pilot of the Bf 109E featured in the photograph left is helped into his kapok-filled life jacket. At this time (1941) JG 27 was operating in Italy. The aircraft shows signs of a recent respray and application of new national markings. The yellow octane triangle has all but disappeared under the new mottle (429/622/32).

Above 1 Gruppe Stab aircraft of ZG 26 in Italy. The machine is a Bf 110E-2 with a yellow-painted nose and patched starboard rudder. Individual aircraft letter B is green outlined in white (422/24/36A).

Below Strangely camouflaged Bf 109E-4 of 2/JG 27 in the Western Desert. Camouflage is an amalgam of several European patterns and would have been predominantly green, which must have stood out against the desert. The ground crew are 'wearing' typical summer dress for the area and appear to be absorbed in a game of cards. The Shell can in the background is worthy of note (435/1003A/27).

Above 7/JG 26 was the first single-engined fighter unit to be transferred to Sicily from Europe. The Staffelkapitan was Joachim Müncheberg whose red heart badge seen on the cowling of this Bf 109E-7 was carried by all 7th Staffel aircraft. This particular Messerschmitt still has the green/grey mottle camouflage associated with Europe, and the cowling is yellow (427/408/4).

Below A quick paint job on the cowling of a Bf 109E-7 of JG 27 (431/710/26A).

Above A 7/JG 26 Bf 109E has a 66 Imperial gallon fuel tank secured to its fuselage rack. The leading edge wing slots of the Bf 109E can be clearly seen on this aircraft (426/383/14).

Below This fighter pilot is securing flares for the flare pistol seen hanging on a lanyard around his neck, before boarding his aircraft somewhere in Italy in 1941. In addition to the early-style life jacket, he is also wearing a one-piece flying suit, which was a little unusual for fighter pilots. The position of the first-aid location mark on the fuselage cross should be compared with the photograph below right (428/485/13A).

Above Refuelling a Bf 109E of I/JG 26. The aircraft formerly belonged to the 7th Staffel whose badge has been removed from the cowling (432/766/32).

Below Joachim Müncheberg and friend (?) with a senior Luftwaffe officer. The position of the first-aid symbol on the removable access panel, when compared with the facing photograph, would seem to indicate that there was no laid-down position for this on the panel concerned. The attachment to the fuselage just above the marking is the insulating point for the aerial (428/481/5A).

Above Green (80) blotched over sand (79) gives a distinctive appearance to this Bf 109E of JG 27 which is lined up for some form of ceremony. The 4 is yellow (04) outlined in black (435/1006A/2A).

Below The massive Daimler Benz DB 605 12-cylinder engine of this Bf 109G-6 produces some quizzical looks from the investigating ground crew (468/1404/23A).

Above right Different sizes and styles of individual markings as well as camouflage patterns are very evident on this trio of Bf 109E-4 Trops of I/JG 27 (431/709/15).

Right Bf 110G-2 with 66 Imperial gallon wing tanks, escorting Ju 52s over the Mediterranean. The aircraft belonged to the 8th Staffel of III/ZG 26 and operated from Sicily (419/1897/9).

Background photograph and right inset
Although strictly speaking not a fighter, the Ju 88
was used in almost every role in World War 2.
This Ju 88A-6/U operated on anti-shipping pat-
rols from Sicily. It is fitted with Fug 200 Hohent-
weil ASV radar and is black underneath. Its top
surfaces are two shades of grey with a wavy line
disruptive pattern (476/2090/5A and
473/1837/23A).

Left inset This Bf 110E-3 3U + LR of the 7th
Staffel of III/ZG 26 is fitted with ETC 50 racks
under the wings and ETC 500 racks under the
fuselage. The dust filter over the carburettor
intake on the port wing outboard of the engine is
clearly visible as is damage to the wing's leading
edge. Spinner is black tipped with white and the
unit badge is red/black checks with white symbols
(443/1578/25A).

This page and above right This is an interesting set of pictures showing the preparation of a Bf 109F-1 Trop of II/JG 27 on a desert landing ground. The Gruppe Badge showing a black bear on a white shield with a black crown over the top can be seen on the cowling of the aircraft which has sand (79) top surfaces and Hellblau (65) under surfaces. The white fuselage band has been painted over the Gruppe symbol and the individual figure 9 is black outlined in white (434/916/7, 10 and 12).

Below Major Schulze-Dickow, Kommandeur of 9/ZG 26, aboard his Bf 110E-3. The Gruppe Kommandeur's badge (in this case III Gruppe) was not usually carried on twin-engined fighters. In this case it has
been painted vertically instead of horizontally and has the 9th Staffel's cockerel superimposed over it
(435/1021/17).

Above The two 7·9 mm MG 15 machine-guns of this Bf 110E-2 of III/ZG 26 receive some attention from two 'blackmen', the slang name given to ground crew because of their overalls. The nose is white and the penguin, which is superimposed over two white chevrons, carries a red umbrella (428/457/23A).

Below Luftwaffe personnel of III/ZG 26 show an Italian officer the rear armament of a Bf 110E-2. The oil-streaked cowling and worn wing root are useful modelling points (422/119/21A).

Above right A Bf 110F-3 has its starboard engine run-up. This photographic reconnaissance aircraft has been fitted with dummy guns, and the two ports below the nose representing outlets for the 20 mm cannon have been painted on (439/1261/37).

Right This appears to be the same aircraft as in the previous photograph, but it is, in fact, a Bf 110C-5. Close study of the two photographs will reveal differences in camouflage, background terrain and under wing markings. This machine is having its cameras loaded prior to a sortie over the desert. Once again its nose armament is dummy (435/1007A/3).

Above A Bf 110F-2 of an unidentified unit attracts a lot of attention from Luftwaffe ground crew whose style of dress shows little uniformity (431/746/36).

Below Setting-up the guns of a JG 26 Bf 109E on a desert firing range. Tail support, removed cowling, and the general odds and ends littered around make this a natural diorama subject for modellers. Note that the aircraft has its flaps partially lowered (431/736/2).

Above right 'Steady does it.' The job of changing a propeller called for careful handling and a lot of labour. This aircraft is a Bf 110E-2 3U + CS of 8/ZG 26. III Gruppe aircraft normally carried the ladybird badge in a white diamond, but this one, whilst retaining the white diamond, has an alternative centre. Nose is white (422/25/34A).

Right View from the radio operator's seat of a Bf 110. A clock, turn and bank indicator, airspeed indicator and altimeter are on the panel before him, and to the right can be seen a compass and morse key, the latter somewhat hidden by the curtain. The handle on the left was used to wind the trailing aerial in or out. This is an aircraft from III/ZG 26 (427/412/9).

Left This Luftwaffe Haupt-mann of a reconnaissance unit (badge above left pocket) samples the spoils of war by downing a bottle of British-brewed Black Horse Ale (785/255/13).

Below A 250 kg bomb on the ETC fuselage rack of a Bf 109E (429/622/20).

Right If you have ever wondered where and by whom certain aircraft painting was carried out, here is the answer. A Gefreiter (Airman first class) applies white paint to the spinner of a JG 27 Bf 109E. I wonder if he matched the colour with laid-down regulations before applying it (431/710/30A).

Below right Sand storms and the extremely cold nights made it essential to keep vital parts of aircraft covered when they were on the ground. This sand (79) camouflaged Hs 126 of 2(H)14 is being secured for the night (431/724/13A).

OVERLEAF

Background photograph This Ju 88D reconnaissance aircraft finished in sand and blue belongs to 1(F)121, and shares its Sicilian base with similar aircraft still carrying European camouflage, and quadrupeds wearing universal camouflage (427/435/2)!

Left inset A Bf 109G-6 of JG 53 being prepared for a sortie from its base in Sicily (473/1837/11A).

Right inset Airfield defence was the responsibility of the Luftwaffe who had their own personnel to carry it out. This patrol, whose truck carries the Afrika Korps palm tree symbol as well as its own squadron marking, seems to have spotted something likely to cause concern (442/1456/31).

Left An Unteroffizier of JG 53 poses before the nose of his Bf 109G. The cannister on the left of his life jacket is the automatic inflation bottle and the tube with the compass is for mouth inflation and/or topping up (473/1837/15A).

Below An Oberleutnant pilot and his gunner board their Bf 110. The gun sight in the forward cockpit, and the removable 57 mm armoured glass over the front windscreen, as well as the rear-view mirror in the opened canopy, are all good points worth noting by the model maker (419/1897/16).

Right A Bf 110F-1 of the Gruppe Adjutant of I/ZG 26. The aircraft has a pair of ETC 500 racks below the fuselage and ETC 50 racks under the wings. It could carry two 550 lb SC 500 general-purpose bombs or SD 250 fragmentation bombs on these racks. The armoured windscreen is not fitted and the port engine cowling has been removed (432/771/21).

Below right FW 190F-8s of I/SG 4 on an Italian airfield. The badge on the nose is a green bomb on a white background ridden by a black Mickey Mouse wielding an axe (479/2176/35).

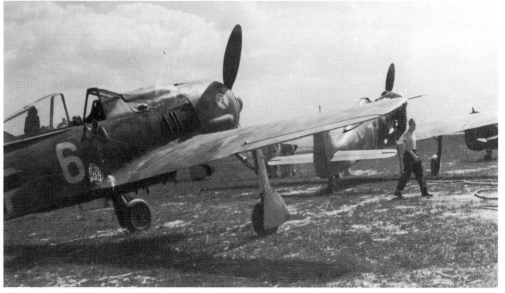

Above and above right Photographs of fighter versions of the FW 190 operating in Italy seem to be comparatively rare. Although these two were included in the files containing Italian- and North African-based units, it seems more likely that they were taken in France or Holland. They are, however, included for general interest (482/2864/30a and 18).

Below left The wide track undercarriage, which made the FW 190 so much easier to handle on the ground than the Bf 109, can be seen to advantage in this head-on view of an unknown unit's aircraft in Italy in 1944 (557/1007/4).

Below The recovery team are probably only interested in usable parts of this FW 190A-8 believed to have belonged to I/JG 3 (466/1395/8A).

Above This Bf 110E-2 of 9/ZG 26 has the Kommandeur's chevrons and white cockerel on its nose. Engine nacelles are painted in the Staffel colour (yellow 04) and the spinners have a white tip separated from the yellow by a black band. Code is 3U + BT (427/442/32).

Below The view from the FW 190's cockpit was not very good when the aircraft was on the ground. It was advisable to have a man 'wing riding' to act as a guide. This F-8 fighter-bomber of I/SG 4 has just returned from a ground-attack mission and is taxiing to its dispersal in Italy (479/2176/18).

Above A Bf 109E-7, probably of JG 27, is rearmed on its desert landing ground. Note the oil-stained undercarriage doors and plugged wing gun (432/760/35).

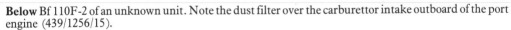

Below Bf 110F-2 of an unknown unit. Note the dust filter over the carburettor intake outboard of the port engine (439/1256/15).

Left A sinister trio pose before a Bf 110F-2 of III/ZG 26. Model makers will find a wealth of detail in this photograph if they take the trouble to study it (428/463/36).

Below left The Fieseler Fl 156 Storch was a popular communications, reconnaissance and artillery-spotting aircraft in every theatre of operations. This one has just brought General Irwin Rommel, centre with cap, to a desert assignment (442/1492/2a).

Above The bleakness of the desert is brought home in this view of a Bf 109E of JG 27 and its attendant truck (431/710/32A).

Below Abandoned P-40 Tomahawk carrying code WR is examined by a Luftwaffe officer. Aircraft has sand and brown top surfaces and azure under surfaces. (416/1659/21).

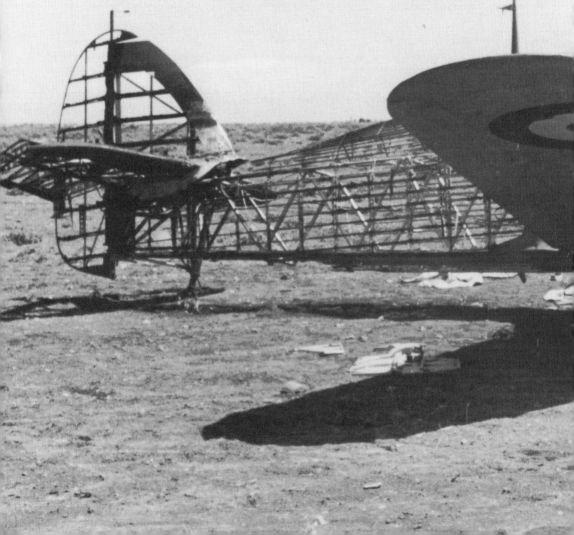

Background photograph The burned-out wreck of a Hurricane appears to bow its nose in temporary submission to the Bf 110 in the background (428/461/22A).

Left inset Bf 109G-6 throws up the dust as it taxies out on its Italian airfield in 1944. The aircraft carries individual code 14 in yellow and a oddly placed III Gruppe symbol in white. The unit is unknown but it might well have been JG 77 (469/1492/28).

Right inset A Lysander complete with bomb racks on its spatted undercarriage is left to the ravages of the desert (428/461/25A).

Above left Another rather forlorn Hurricane whose starboard wing guns have been removed. Examination of the print under a magnifying glass reveals one bullet hole almost dead centre of the windscreen (431/716/18A).

Left and this page These three photographs are interesting as they show a badge which belonged to a so far unknown but apparently very prophetical unit, since they chose EFTA as part of their legend. The aircraft is a Bf 108 Taifun which was a popular communications machine, examples of which are still flying today. Camouflage is sand (79) with green blotches and blue under surfaces; 'Taifun' is in white. The photographs were taken in Sardinia (434/932/10, 14 and 18).

Above Hs 129B-1 ground-support aircraft on a road near Tripoli in 1942. Captions in other publications have claimed this aircraft to be getting ready to take off, but close examination shows both engine cowlings removed and a steering yoke attached to the rear wheel. Aircraft belongs to 8/SG 2 (419/1878/3).

Below The 'headless' armourer could be an apt title for this shot of a Bf 109G-6's 21 cm rocket-launching tubes. The figure looking quizzically down the front end is a Feldwebel (Sergeant) (469/1492/16).

Above Bf 109F-2 of Oberleutnant Hans-Joachim Marseille of JG 27 being refuelled. The red rudder carries 48 kill markings which dates the photograph around February 24 1942 as it was on this day he recorded his 48th victory and was awarded the Knight's Cross (439/1273/33).

Below The belt of .303 ammunition seems to indicate that this Hurricane was caught before it could give an account of itself. The long-range tanks would have given it a tremendous disadvantage in air to air combat and the fact that the gear is down and there is very little damage could well indicate that it did not fall into Luftwaffe hands as a result of combat (434/915/11).

This page Bf 110F-3 of AuflGr 14 being prepared for operations with its crew watching the ground crew run up the engines. The positions are then reversed as the mechanic watches the aircraft move out for take-off (431/743/16 and 22).

Right Rubber boots seem to be a most inappropriate dress for the desert, none the less they are chosen by the figure on the left of this trio who are working on a Bf 109E of JG 26. The red heart on the cowling is practically worn away, which could indicate that the aircraft has been transferred from the 7th Staffel, or time has not been available to repaint it (432/760/28).

Below right Bf 109G of I/JG 77 makes its final approach to an Italian airfield (468/1414/11A).

Left The famous spiral spinner decoration much favoured by Luftwaffe fighter pilots appeared everywhere, including the desert. It is shown here on a Bf 109G-2 of III/JG 27 whose badge can be seen on the cowling (469/1458/24).

Below The Me 210 was not a resounding success but was used in the Mediterranean for a short time. This Me 210A-1 coded 2N + CD, photographed in Tunisia, carries the clog emblem of II/ZG 26 on its engine cowlings, although the letter D would indicate that it was a Stab aircraft of III Gruppe/ZG 76. II/ZG 26 was formed from III/ZG 76 which might explain the apparent anomaly (421/2051/19).

Right The pilot of 2N + CD leaving his Me 210A-1. The lightweight flying suit, life jacket and seemingly cramped cockpit are of interest. The code was previously used by Versuchstaffel 210 of Gruppe Stab III/ZG 1 (421/2052/24A).

Below right The same Me 210A-1 shown in the previous photo having its guns aligned in the butts (421/2052/23a).

OVERLEAF

Background photograph
Line-up of Bf 109G-6s of I/JG
77. The variety of finishes is
interesting as is the small size
and position of the individual
aircraft figures, although the
latter was not too uncommon in
1944 (468/1421/27).

Left inset Undercarriage retrac-
tion test on a Bf 109E-4 of I/JG
27 in Sicily. Another interesting
diorama topic for modellers
(431/712/14).

Right inset Pause for a smoke
whilst Storch KH + WY waits
with its engine running. Note
the armour column in the background (438/1189/14A).

Left Forward vision from the Bf 109 was not good when the aircraft was on the ground. This is clearly illustrated by the G version of I/JG 77 (468/1414/22a).

Right The Me 410 followed the ill-fated Me 210 and had a little more success. This example is an A-3 probably of 2(F)122 and appears to be creating a great deal of interest (476/2083/8A).

Page 15 and below Two views of an Me 410B-1 photographed in May 1944. The rear firing barbettes, method of canopy opening and the soft demarcation line between the colours on the spinners, are all worthy of noting (483/2833/14 and 20A).

Below right A very pleasing picture of a Bf 109E of JG 27 having its fuselage guns zeroed-in on the butts (435/1014A/25).

Left Luftwaffe mottle camouflage can be seen to good effect on the fuselage of this Gruppe Kommandeur's aircraft. The marking in the centre of the smaller V is a removable panel. Canopy hinging and retaining is interesting (431/707/29).

Below Generalfeldmarschall Kesselring, who commanded Luftflotte 2 and was C in C of all German forces in the Mediterranean area, before his Heinkel He 111. The officer to his right has a Hauptmann's rank insignia on his flight jacket (438/1161/14A).

Right The Oberleutnant on the right throws up a salute to the Oberst who has just left the Luftwaffe vehicle presumably on some form of inspection. The two styles of uniform are worthy of comparison (552/818/10).

Below right The interior of Hans-Joachim Marseille's tent in the desert. The huge spider in its web seems to match the personality of the German pilot who himself was a very patient hunter (445/1872/6).

Above left Like all fighting men Luftwaffe personnel retained a sense of humour whatever conditions they faced. It could not have been too pleasant living in a tent in the desert. This decorated example shows a tendency to knock at authority as well as record current events (439/1287/10).

Left Pilots of JG 53 in Sicily. The Oberfeldwebel on the right has his flares around his waist and the Leutnant next to him is wearing a late-issue zippered flight jacket (420/2030/36A).

Above Destroyed Ju 52s and Me 110s on a desert airfield (432/767/29).

Right One way of keeping the Italian sun from making the cockpit too hot. Aircraft is a Bf 109G-6 of JG 77 (469/1456/7A).

Left The Leutnant on the wing adjusts his camera prior to taking a snapshot of the pilot standing behind him for the squadron album. The early-style kapok life jacket and flight trousers date this photograph to about 1941. The standing pilot is holding a screwdriver in his right hand which might indicate a mechanical bent as far as either the camera or the Bf 109E is concerned (428/482/21A).

Right The familiar face of Adolf Galland on the right as he meets Oberst Lützow in Italy. The leather gloves worn by all three men seem a little incongruous with the summer dress (468/1421/31).

Right The lightweight flying helmet and survival compass of this JG 53 pilot are shown to advantage in this study of man and his best friend (415/1646/25A).

OVERLEAF

Background photograph Any aircraft taking off in the desert left a tell-tale trail of dust and sand as can be seen in this photograph of four Bf 109s of JG 27 scrambling from their desert strip (435/1003A/6).

Above inset Bf 109G of II/JG 77 and a Macchi MC 205V of 1° Gruppo fly over inhospitable terrain in 1943 (470/1681/8A).

Below inset Forty-three kill markings on the rudder of a Bf 109E in North Africa. The circles above the marks contain dates and types of victim (431/707/20).

Above An Oberfeldwebel pilot and colleague discuss tactics with the Italian pilot of this Macchi MC 205 of 72° Squadriglia, 77° Gruppo, 1° Stormo. The 1° Stormo badge is on the white band and the forward badge is the fasces insignia (466/1394/3).

Below Macchi MC 200 Saetta carrying the badge of 4° Stormo on its white fuselage band. The cowling is yellow and camouflage is a green wave pattern over a sand base. The cockpit flap and very small radio aerial are noteworthy (430/677/31).

Above The desolation of the desert is brought home in this photograph which shows oil drums marking the road. In the event of a sand storm these drums should still be apparent (431/710/21).

Below Home Sweet Home. Pilots of JG 27 relax in front of their living quarters, somewhere in North Africa (445/1899/34).

Background photograph Line-up of Macchi MC 205 fighter aircraft of 1° Stormo in Sicily, 1943. The aircraft have sand blotched with green upper surfaces and light grey undersides (466/1392/26).

Left inset MC 205V of 1° Gruppo. It carries the tricolour markings of the RSI on the fuselage and fin, and could well be in the hands of a Luftwaffe pilot. The aircraft on the left has been repainted with German markings (470/1681/26A).

Right inset A Macchi MC 202 of 155° Gruppo lands on its airfield which is also the home of Bf 109Gs of II/JG 51 (468/1415/9).

Above This MC 200 Saetta belongs to 373° Squadriglia of the 153° Gruppo, 53° Stormo and was seen in Libya in December 1941. Fuselage insignia is the Ace of Clubs (436/1026/36).

Below The Macchi MC205V was powered by a licence-built DB 605 12-cylinder engine and it was one of the few Axis fighters with an all-round performance equal to those operated by the Allies. This is an aircraft of 1° Stormo in Sicily in 1943 and is in the same bomb-proof dispersals as those in the background photograph on pages 80 and 81 (466/1392/30).

Above This is an early-production MC 200 and was probably photographed in Sicily in June 1940. The underwing fasces are white on black instead of the normal black on white (422/32/36A).

Below There is an air of nonchalance among the Italian ground crew watching this CR 42 having its guns zeroed. The Italian biplane was extremely manoeuvrable and a joy to fly, but it could not match the firepower or speed of its German and British contemporaries (435/1014A/29).

Left Italian pilot climbs aboard his MC 202 Folgore in Libya in July 1942. The camouflage pattern is particularly clear on this photograph (466/1392/31).

Above Both the Luftwaffe motorcyclist and Arab donkey rider look to be pointing in the direction of take-off as indicated by the striped windsock on this JG 27 desert landing ground (786/343/15).

Right Finding the way in the desert was just as important as in the air. A sun compass fitted to the wing of this vehicle was one method of keeping a check on the direction being travelled (434/921/12).

Above Fighter pilots of JG 77 based in Italy listen to a colleague describing his latest success (428/478/3A).

Below The cowling and spatted undercarriage of this Ju 87 make a suitable frame for the graveyard of several Hurricanes (435/1008/20).

Right Italian pilot of a CR 42 biplane fighter takes the sun in the traditional manner. The black/white underwing fasces are clearly visible (435/1014A/35).

Background photograph A typical Luftwaffe desert landing ground, with two aircraft in the circuit and a pair at dispersal (435/1003A/24).

Inset Personnel of Luftwaffe airfield defence units at a field briefing (77/18/14A).

Left The leather greatcoat of Major Hartlaub makes a strange contrast with the desert dress of the other two officers (77/17/13A).

Below far left Major Janke, photographed on February 4 1942 when he was serving with JG 51 (444/1662/3).

Below left Oberleutnant Klaus Buetschneider showing typical Luftwaffe uniform and badges. His rank epaulettes and collar badges are those of an Oberleutnant which was a rank equivalent to Flying Officer. His unit was not known when this photograph was taken but he went on to serve with JG 300 (74/1416/36).

Right Oberfeldwebel Schultz. This rank is equivalent to Flight Sergeant and is shown by two pips on a yellow (aircrew) backed epaulette. It is normally supported by collar patches showing four eagles. The badges on his left pocket look to be an aircrew badge to the left and a air gunner's to the right, but this is by no means certain (440/1303/6).

Below An alternative style of dress for Oberleutnant Joachim Müncheberg. He is wearing a leather flight jacket on which he carries only rank epaulettes. His dress cap was junior officers' summer wear (435/1016A/31).

Below right Leutnant Hans Sauer, a fighter pilot from Bonn showing his Knight's Cross and display ribbon (432/762/12).

Left The one-piece flying suit worn by bomber crews in the early days of World War 2 and on some occasions by single-seat fighter pilots. Bf 110 crews often wore the suit but by mid-1942 it was very rare in the Mediterranean theatre (449/752/19).

Below Oberleutnant Dietrich, the pilot of a reconnaissance aircraft serving in North Africa. The clasp above his left pocket is a reconnaissance qualification badge (444/1662/5).

Right He 111 torpedo bombers operating from Sicily and Italy required fighter escort over the hostile Mediterranean, especially when they operated within fighter range of Malta. This aircraft of an unknown unit awaits its tin-fish (449/759/10).

Below right A tranquil scene in Italy as a Bf 109G-5 of JG 77 awaits its next call to duty (421/2070/21).

1. Fighter units and their aircraft used in the Mediterranean and North Africa

III/ZG 26	Bf 110 C–4, Bf 110E–1, Me 210A–1.
7/JG 26	Bf 109E–7 Trop, Bf109F–4.
Stab JG 27	Bf 109F–4 Trop.
I, II, III/ JG 27	Bf 109F–4 Trop.
Jabo JG 27	Bf 109F–4B.
I/JG 27	Bf 109E–7 Trop.
Stab JG 53	Bf 109F–4 Trop, Bf 109G–6 Trop.
I/JG 53	Bf 109F–4 Trop, Bf 109G–6 Trop.
II/JG 53	Bf 109F–4 Trop, Bf 109G–6 Trop.
III/JG 53	Bf 109F–4 Trop, Bf 109G–6 Trop.
I/NJG 2	Ju 88C–4.
2/NJG 2	Ju 88C–6.
4/NJG 2	Ju 88C–4.
7/ZG 26	Bf 110D.
9/Zg 26	Bf 110D.
Stab JG 77	Bf 109G–6 Trop.
I/JG 77	Bf 109G–6 Trop.
SKG 10	Various elements all with FW 190A5 fighter bombers.
II/JG 51	Bf 109F–4.
II/JG 2	FW 190A–4.
II/JG 2	Bf 109G–2.
II/JG 3	Bf 109F–4.
II/JG 26	Bf 109G–2.

---

2. Luftwaffe fighters used in the Middle East

Messerschmitt Bf 109F–4 Trop
Span:	32 feet $6\frac{1}{2}$ inches. Length: 29 feet $\frac{1}{2}$ inch.
Engine:	Tropicalised Daimler-Benz DB601E 12-cylinder, inverted V, 1,300 hp.
Performance:	Maximum speed 390 mph at 22,000 feet; cruising speed 310 mph at 16,000 feet. Service ceiling 37,000 feet.
Armament:	One 20 mm MG 151 cannon with 200 rounds, and two 7·9 mm MG 17 machine-guns with 500 rpg.

Messerschmitt Me 210A–1
Span:	53 feet $7\frac{3}{4}$ inches. Length: 36 feet $8\frac{1}{4}$ inches.
Engines:	Two Daimler-Benz DB 601F 12-cylinder, inverted V, 1,395 hp each.
Performance:	Maximum speed 385 mph at 20,000 feet; cruising speed 290 mph at 15,000 feet. Service ceiling 22,965 feet.
Armament:	Two 20 mm MG 151 cannon, two 7·9 mm MG 17 and two remotely controlled 13 mm MG 131 machine-guns in fuselage mounted barbettes.

Messerschmitt Bf 110C–4
Span:	53 feet $4\frac{3}{4}$ inches. Length: 39 feet $8\frac{1}{2}$ inches.
Engines:	Two Daimler-Benz DB 601A 12-cylinder, inverted V, 1,100 hp each.
Armament:	Four 7·9 mm MG 17 machine-guns, two 20 mm MG FF cannon all firing forward, and usually one 7·9 mm MG 15 for rearward defence.

Other titles in the same series

No 1 Panzers in the desert
by Bruce Quarrie

No 2 German bombers over England
by Bryan Philpott

No 3 Waffen-SS in Russia
by Bruce Quarrie

No 4 Fighters defending the Reich
by Bryan Philpott

No 5 Panzers in North-West Europe
by Bruce Quarrie

In preparation

No 7 German paratroops in the Med
by Bruce Quarrie

No 8 German bombers over Russia
by Bryan Philpott

No 9 Panzers in Russia
by Bruce Quarrie

No 10 German fighters over England
by Bryan Philpott

Plus many more!

ACHTUNG! COMPLETED YOUR COLLECTION?

Thank you for buying this **AZTEX** book. We're sure you will find it informative and enjoyable. If you would like to be kept informed of the publishing dates of future titles please send your name and address to:

Announcements
Dept WWII
AZTEX Corporation
P O Box 50046
Tucson, AZ 85703